paper
magic

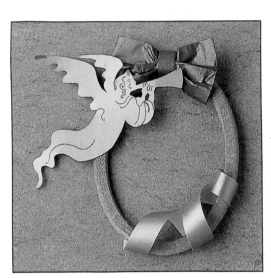

paper magic

60 origami and papercaft designs

paul jackson

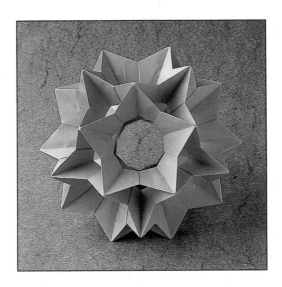

southwater

This edition is published by Southwater

Southwater is an imprint of Anness Publishing Ltd
Hermes House, 88–89 Blackfriars Road, London SE1 8HA
tel. 020 7401 2077; fax 020 7633 9499; info@anness.com

© Anness Publishing Ltd 1999, 2002

Published in the USA by Southwater, Anness Publishing Inc.
27 West 20th Street, New York, NY 10011; fax 212 807 6813

This edition distributed in the UK by The Manning Partnership
251–253 London Road East, Batheaston, Bath BA1 7RL
tel. 01225 852 727; fax 01225 852 852; sales@manning-partnership.co.uk

This edition distributed in the USA by National Book Network
4720 Boston Way, Lanham, MD 20706
tel. 301 459 3366; fax 301 459 1705; www.nbnbooks.com

This edition distributed in Canada by General Publishing
895 Don Mills Road, 400–402 Park Centre, Toronto, Ontario M3C 1W3
tel. 416 445 3333; fax 416 445 5991; www.genpub.com

This edition distributed in Australia by Sandstone Publishing
Unit 1, 360 Norton Street, Leichhardt, New South Wales 2040
tel. 02 9560 7888; fax 02 9560 7488; sales@sandstonepublishing.com.au

This edition distributed in New Zealand by The Five Mile Press (NZ) Ltd
PO Box 33-1071 Takapuna, Unit 11/101-111 Diana Drive, Glenfield, Auckland 10
tel. (09) 444 4144; fax (09) 444 4518; fivemilenz@clear.net.nz

A CIP catalogue record for this book is available from the British Library.

Publisher: Joanna Lorenz
Project Editor: Fiona Eaton
Designer: Lilian Lindblom
Photographer: Martin Norris
Contributors: Angela A'Court, Marion Elliot
Illustrators: Anna Koska, Lorraine Harrison

Previously published as *Origami & Papercraft*

1 3 5 7 9 10 8 6 4 2

CONTENTS

INTRODUCTION

Paper is everywhere: our lives would be impossible without wrappings, letters, magazines, cards, packaging, leaflets, posters, newspapers and notepads. It is inexpensive and readily available, and as an art and craft material it is infinitely adaptable. Using the ancient art of origami, a sheet of paper can be turned into a host of ingenious and surprising shapes: our easy-to-follow sequences will guide you into an irresistible world of magical transformations. Add scissors and glue, ribbons and paints, and your own imagination and enthusiasm, and you can use the ideas shown in this book to transform all kinds of paper into fantastic gifts, original stationery and beautiful decorations.

ORIGAMI

You can have fun with origami anywhere, any time: all you need is a sheet of paper and a firm surface to work on. These projects are arranged in order of difficulty, so if you are a beginner try the simple ones first and don't be too ambitious too soon. For extra help on the basics, you can refer to the section on Origami Techniques. The easiest and cheapest source of good quality practice paper is photocopy (Xerox) paper. For two-tone models, coloured origami paper is ideal, but patterned gift-wrap paper is a good alternative. Here are a few guidelines to help make the process of folding easier and more satisfying:

- Check that the paper you are folding is exactly square.
- Do not try to fold against a soft surface, such as a carpet or your lap: rest the paper on a table or board.
- Crease slowly, firmly and accurately, especially when making the early creases.
- The instructions and symbols on one step will create a shape which looks like the next step but stripped of its symbols. So, always look ahead to the next step to see what shape you are trying to make.

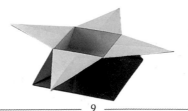

GLIDER

This design is one of a number of similar gliders of Chinese origin,
all of which fly extremely well.

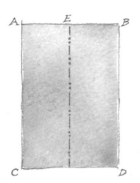

1 Fold the sheet in half down the middle, as a mountain fold. Unfold.

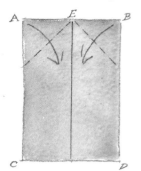

2 Fold in corners A & B to the centre crease.

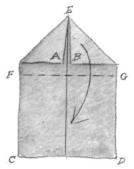

3 Fold down E along crease FG. Note that FG is a little below the level of AB.

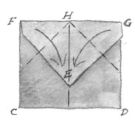

4 Fold in corners F & G, leaving E exposed.

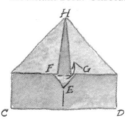

5 Fold up E over F & G.

6 Mountain fold D to C.

7 Before creasing, press flat the existing creases. Then, make the wing creases from the nose tip at H. To fly the glider, hold as shown at the point of balance, and release smoothly but firmly.

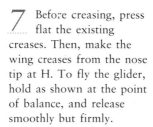

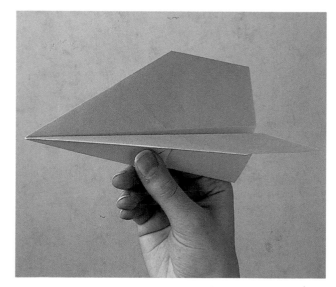

CANDY BAG

*If folded from greaseproof paper, this practical design will hold fries
and other oily or sticky foods. For extra strength, fold two squares
together. For sweets or candies, use any paper, not too thin.*

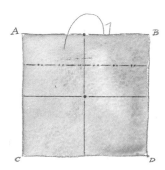

1 Fold and unfold
the paper in half
horizontally and vertically.
Mountain fold edge AB to
the centre crease.

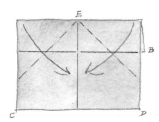

2 Fold in the top corners
to the centre crease.

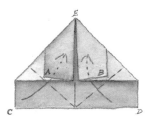

3 Similarly, fold in
bottom corners
C & D, but tucking them
beneath A & B, to lock
them flat.

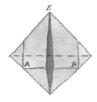

4 Valley fold in half
across the middle,
then . . .

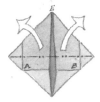

5 . . . mountain fold
in half, to create a
flexible crease. Open out
the bag.

6 The Candy Bag
complete.

BUTTERFLY

*There are a great many origami butterflies in all manner of styles, some
very complex. This is one of the simplest. It is important to use origami
paper, so that white triangles appear at the edges between the coloured
wings, to separate them visually. Cut a square of origami paper in half to
create a 2 x 1 rectangle. Start coloured side up.*

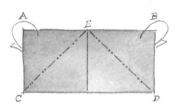

1 Fold corners A & B behind to the centre.

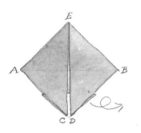

2 Fold EC & ED to the centre crease, allowing corners A & B to flip outwards . . .

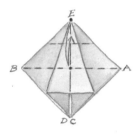

3 . . . like this. Compare the position of the lettered corners with their position in Step 2. Turn over.

4 First, crease from B to A, across the middle. Then, fold E to the centre point.

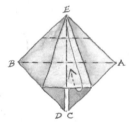

5 Re-form the Step 4 creases, but this time tuck E up under the horizontal edge.

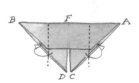

6 With vertical creases that run inside up to edge BA, mountain fold the loose corners behind as far as they will go.

7 Make a mountain and two valley creases where shown, to create the body and to swivel points D & C apart.

8 The Butterfly complete.

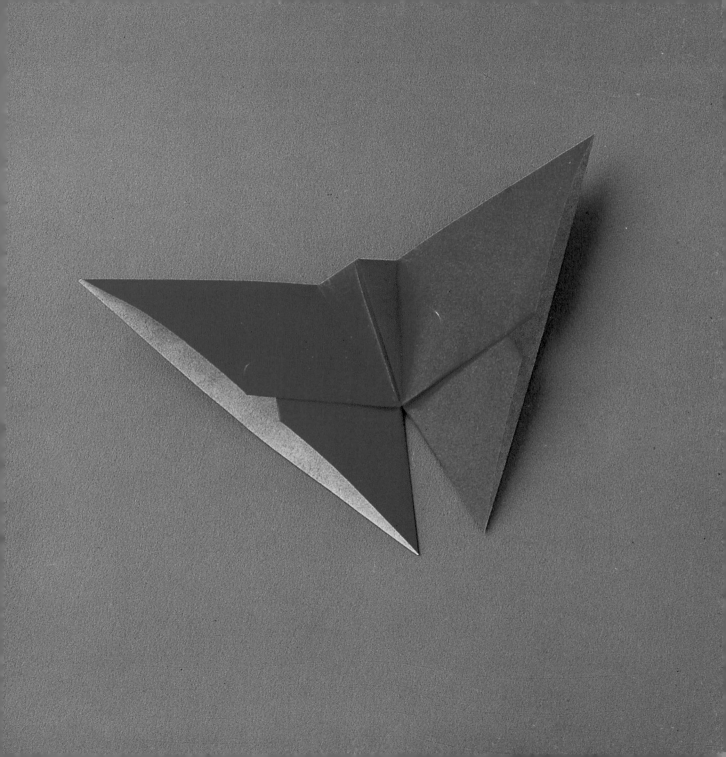

SAMPAN

*This is a simplified version of a sampan with a canopy over each end of the boat.
Both designs feature an extraordinary move – here shown in Steps 7–9 – in which
the entire shape is turned inside out. With a little extra folding, one end of the
sampan can be blunted to create a rowing boat. Use a square of paper.
If using origami paper, start coloured side up.*

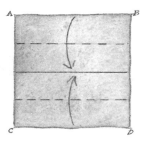

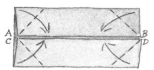

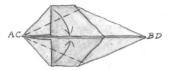

1 Crease and unfold across the centre. Fold the top and bottom edges to the crease.

2 Fold in the corners.

3 Narrow the corner at the right, as though making the familiar paper dart.

4 Repeat at the left, overlapping the Step 4 creases.

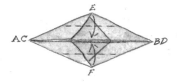

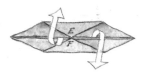

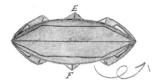

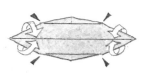

5 Fold in E & F to the centre crease. The paper is thick, so press firmly.

6 Open out all the layers revealing the coloured base . . .

7 . . . like this, to form a loose boat shape. Turn over.

8 To lock the sampan, push down on the four arrowed corners, so that the whole of the structure inverts and turns inside out!

9 The Sampan complete.

DUCK STEP

Napkin folds always create a point of interest on a dining table.
The Duck Step is a basic form from which other varieties
of napkin fold can be made.

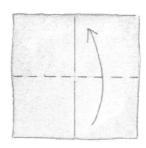

1 Completely unfold
a napkin, then fold the
bottom edge up to the top.

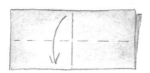

2 Fold the top edge
down to the crease.

3 Fold each half of the
top edge down the
centre crease . . .

4 . . . like this. Turn the
napkin over.

5 Mountain fold the
right side behind
the left.

6 Valley fold the front
square up over the
triangle. Repeat behind.

7 The Duck Step napkin
complete.

CABLE BUFFET

The Cable Buffet server allows guests at a buffet or picnic to help themselves to food, a napkin and cutlery all at once.

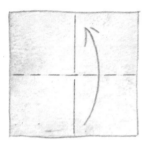

1 Completely unfold a napkin, then fold the bottom edge up to the top.

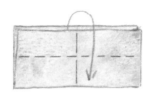

2 Fold the top layer down to the crease.

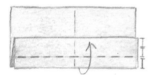

3 Fold the top layer back up a little way . . .

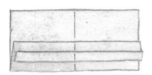

4 . . . like this. Turn the napkin over.

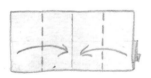

5 Fold the sides to the middle.

6 Tuck one half deep into the other, locking the napkin flat.

7 The Cable Buffet server complete. Insert cutlery into the pocket ready for the meal.

BISHOP

The elegant curves and free-standing structure of this folded napkin create a strong impact on any table.

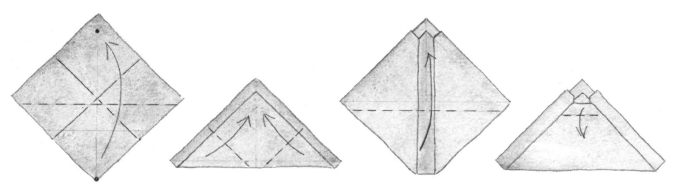

1 Completely unfold a napkin, then fold the bottom corner almost up to the top.

2 Fold up the bottom corners to the position shown in Step 3.

3 Fold up the bottom corner to the position shown in Step 4.

4 Fold down the front edge.

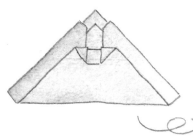  

5 This is the basic shape. The proportions are important, so it may be necessary to adjust some of the folds. Turn the napkin over.

6 Bend the left and right halves forward. Interlock one half into the other to make a tube that will not spring open.

7 The Bishop napkin complete.

FISH

This fish is pre-creased and collapsed into shape. When pre-creasing,
it is important to fold accurately (here, up to Step 5), otherwise the creases
will not fall into place to achieve Step 6. For extra flatness, a speck of glue
inside the mouth will close the layers.

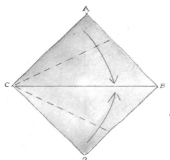

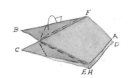

1 Crease and unfold the two diagonals, then bring edges CA & CD to the centre crease CB . . .

2 . . . like this. Unfold them.

3 Similarly, bring edges BA & BD to the centre crease. Unfold.

4 Connect the creases made in Steps 2–3 with mountain and valley creases, as shown. Be careful to place them accurately.

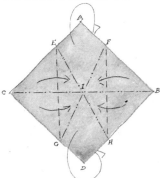

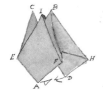

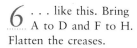

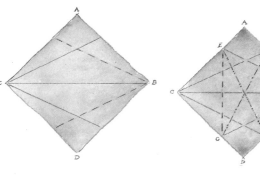

5 Collapse the paper along all the marked creases, noting which are mountains and which are valleys . . .

6 . . . like this. Bring A to D and F to H. Flatten the creases.

7 Lock by pleating one half of the tail fin into the body with a mountain fold and the other with a valley.

8 The Fish complete. Suspend it from a thread attached just behind the top corner at the point of balance.

SLEEPY DOG

The design is simple to make, but it is important to place C accurately in Steps 1 and 2. Once Step 3 has been achieved, the remaining folds fall naturally into place. Note the way in which the eyes are suggested. Use a square of origami paper, coloured side up.

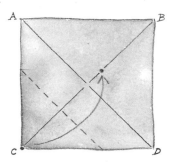

1 Crease and unfold the two diagonals, then fold in corner C to the point described in Step 2.

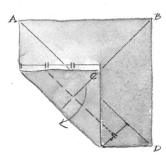

2 Note the position of C. Fold C back out, adding an extra crease as marked.

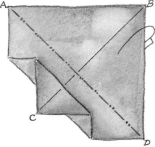

3 Mountain fold B behind, along the AD diagonal.

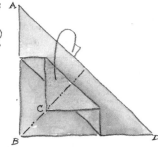

4 Mountain fold A behind to touch D.

5 Fold back points D & A to the outside.

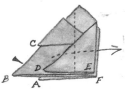

6 With a reverse fold, swing B through the middle. Note the position of the crease.

7 Mountain fold E behind. Repeat at F behind. Turn D, A & C inside out. Fold B forward. Curve the edge at the eye. Repeat for other eye.

8 The Sleepy Dog complete.

MODULAR DECORATION I

*A modular design is one in which a number of identical units are folded,
then locked together without glue to create a geometric form.*

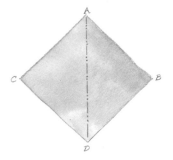

1 With a small square, mountain fold down the diagonal.

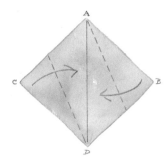

2 Fold in edges AB & CD to the crease.

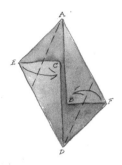

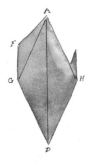

3 Fold in short edges AE & DF to the centre.

4 Mountain fold from A to D.

5 Unfold a little.

6 The module complete. Make four: two of one colour and two of another.

ASSEMBLY

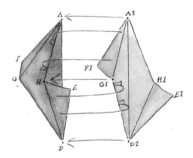

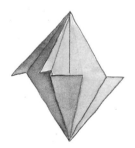

1 Edge A1, F1 on the right-hand module is tucked behind edge AH on the left-hand module. At the same time, edge DE on the left-hand module is tucked behind edge D1, G1 on the right-hand module. Note that A1 touches A, G1 touches H and D1 touches D.

2 This is the result. The lock is not strong, but when two other modules are locked in, so that the fourth locks into the first to close the circle, the complete structure will lock well.

3 The Modular Decoration complete. Suspend the finished module from a thread.

COLOUR CHANGE BIRD

The simple shape of the completed bird and the effectiveness of the colour contrasts are achieved by a fluent and concise sequence of folds. Perhaps it is too stylized for some people, but less can sometimes be more. Use a square of origami paper, white side up.

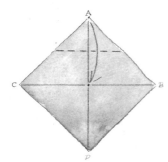

1 Crease and unfold the two diagonals, then fold corner A to the centre point.

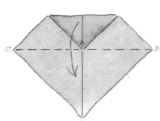

2 Roll the triangle downwards, along crease CB.

3 Fold C & B dot to dot, as shown.

4 Unfold C & B.

5 Turn over.

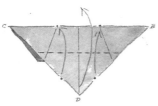

6 Fold dot to dot, aligning edges DC & DB with the tops of the creases made in Step 3.

7 Pull out corner A.

8 Fold down A, level with the folded edge.

9 Fold B behind.

10 Fold up B & C along existing internal (hidden) creases made in Step 3.

11 Reverse fold D to create the head. Fold out the feet to create a stable base for the bird.

12 The Colour Change Bird complete.

MODULAR DECORATION II

The basic modules are very simple to make, but some thought must be given to assembling them correctly. Once locked, they will hold together very well.

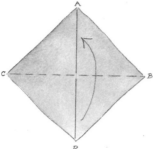

1 Crease and fold a vertical diagonal, then fold D up to A.

2 Fold edge AD,B forward to the vertical crease (valley fold) and edge AD,C behind to that crease (mountain fold).

3 This is the completed module. Make another.

ASSEMBLY

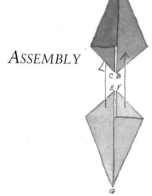

1 Take careful note of the lettered corners. Bring the two modules together, so that F is on top of B, and C is on top of E . . .

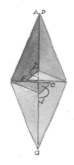

2 . . . like this. Fold F across to the horizontal. Repeat with C, then with E & B behind.

3 Lock the modules together by tucking F & C behind the vertical edges. Repeat behind with E & B.

4 Separate the modules by twisting one away from the other, so that they lie perpendicular to each other. Suspend the completed module from a thread.

HOUSE

Here is a remarkable sequence of three multiform designs which are all made from the same basic shape, the House. The designs shown here are not the full set: it is also possible to fold a dustpan, purse, fox puppet, crown . . . and very probably many others! Experiment by folding the paper this way and that to see what you can discover. Use a square of origami paper, white side up.

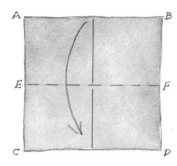

1 Crease and unfold down the middle of a square, then fold AB down to CD.

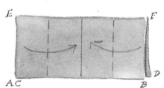

2 Fold the edges to the centre.

3 Unfold.

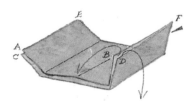

4 Lift up the edge BD,F. Separate B from D, applying pressure on the edges below F . . .

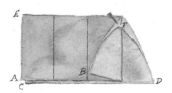

5 . . . like this. Pull B & D right apart and squash F flat.

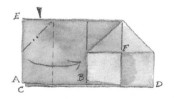

6 Repeat Steps 4–5 on the left, separating A from C and squashing E flat. Let A touch B.

7 The House complete. Children like to draw windows and a door to finish the design.

3D HOUSE

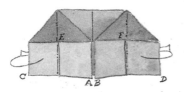

1 Complete Steps 1–6 of the House (see pages 30–1). Fold C & D behind.

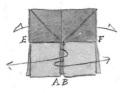

2 Unfold AC & BD.

3 The 3D House complete.

G.I. CAP

To make a full-size cap, use a square trimmed from a large format newspaper.

1 Begin with Step 2 of the 3D House (see page 32). Fold AB up to EF. Repeat behind.

2 Fold up the bottom section along crease EF. Repeat behind.

3 Open out the cap.

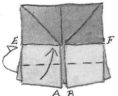

4 The G.I. Cap complete.

STAR

*The shape made in Step 7 is known in origami as the Preliminary Base,
so called because other, more advanced bases can be developed from it,
including the Bird and Frog bases. Use a square of paper or perhaps
paper-backed foil, coloured side up.*

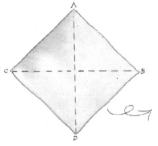

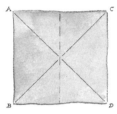

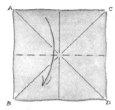

1 Crease and unfold both diagonals as valleys. Turn over.

2 Check that the diagonals are now mountain creases.

3 Fold and unfold in half down the middle, then . . .

4 . . . fold in half across the middle.

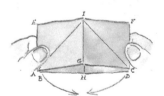

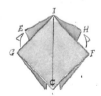

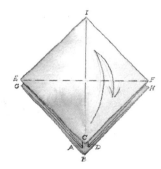

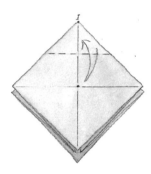

5 Hold as shown. If the mountain and valley creases have been placed correctly, a 3D diamond shape will emerge when the hands are swung towards each other . . .

6 . . . like this. Flatten G against E and F against H.

7 Fold the single layer corner C up to I, then unfold.

8 Fold I down to the centre point. Unfold. Open the paper a little.

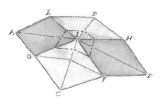

9 The crease formed in Step 8 makes a square. Crease the four sides of the square as mountains . . .

10 . . . like this. Flatten the centre square, then push it downwards into the paper . . .

11 . . . like this. Re-form the Step 8 shape, but with I now sunk inside the paper.

12 Fold up C again.

13 Swing C down to corner G, whilst also bringing corner F across to touch G. The crease from G is a mountain.

14 Halfway.

15 Complete. Note how F, C, G & E lie one behind the other.

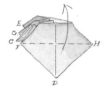

16 Similarly, fold up D along line FH . . .

17 . . . swing towards corner F, bringing H across to touch corner F. Repeat this sequence with A then B, turning the paper over and around each time. Fan out the points in a symmetrical pattern.

WATERBOMB

Many people – particularly mischievous children – have learnt how to make a waterbomb, but without practice it is very easy to forget how to lock it. Without a good lock, it cannot contain the water it is designed to hold!

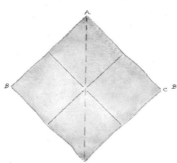

1 Mountain fold horizontally and vertically across the paper. Unfold each time.

2 Form a vertical valley diagonal (the other creases are mountains). Unfold.

3 Fold A down to D.

4 Hold as shown. If the mountains and valleys have been placed correctly, the paper will form a 3D pyramid when the hands are swung towards each other . . .

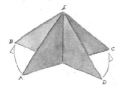

5 . . . like this. Flatten A against B, and D against C.

6 Fold A & C up to E. Repeat behind with B & D. (Note: to increase the size of the hole through which air is blown to inflate the Waterbomb, fold the corners short of E. A hole that is too small is difficult to blow through.)

7 Fold G & H to the centre. Repeat behind.

8 Fold A & C into the centre at G & H.

9 Valley fold the small triangle above A into the pocket made by separating the layers above G. Repeat with C on the right and twice more behind with B and D.

10 The Waterbomb is now locked, front and back. Blow into the hole at the bottom to make it 3D. If the hole is too small, enlarge it.

11 The Waterbomb complete.

TRADITIONAL BOX

*This is perhaps the classic origami box. It is quick and simple to make,
and locks strongly. A box made from a slightly larger square will form a lid.
In Step 3, if the creases are not placed at the quarter points, but elsewhere,
taller or squatter boxes can be made. Use a square of strong paper.
If using origami paper, start white side up.*

1 Mountain fold horizontally and vertically across the centre, unfolding each time.

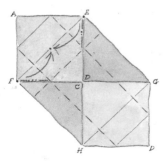

5 Re-crease valleys where shown.

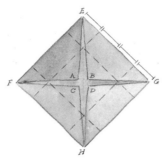

2 Fold the corners to the centre. (The existing creases are mountains.)

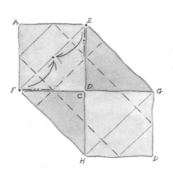

6 Make the paper 3D by bringing F & E to the centre dot . . .

3 Fold each edge in turn to the centre point, unfolding each crease before making the next.

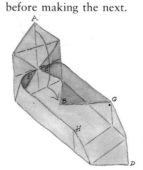

7 . . . like this. Lock the end of the box by folding A over the top and into the middle.

4 Pull open corners A & D.

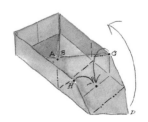

8 Repeat Steps 6–7 with H & G, folding D over the top to lock.

NESTING BIRD

The design features a peculiar and little-used manoeuvre at Steps 4–5, when one spike is pulled out from inside another that envelops it. The move is very satisfying! Begin with a square of paper, same colour both sides.

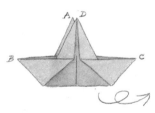

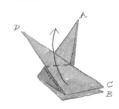

1 Crease and unfold a vertical diagonal, then fold D up to A.

2 Fold edges AD,B and AD,C to the centre crease.

3 Fold out corners B & C.

4 Note the shape of the paper. Pull out D from inside A . . .

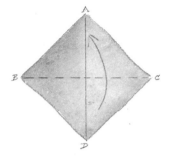

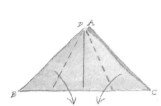

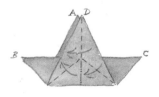

5 . . . like this. Flatten D on top of A.

6 Turn over.

7 Collapse the paper as shown, separating A from D and bringing C to touch B.

8 Lift up corner C, squashing the paper flat at the left.

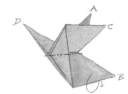

9 Fold B behind.

10 Reverse fold D. Fold out the bottom corners to stay away from the wings and so create a stable base for the bird to balance on.

BEAK

This is a variation on a well-known origami "action" theme.
The mechanism will be familiar to knowledgeable paper folders, but here
the eyes are made differently. It is important to use origami paper,
to achieve a contrast of colour for the eyes and the inside of the mouth.

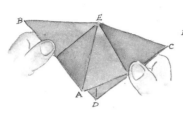 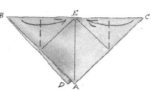 

1 Begin with Step 4 of the Waterbomb project (see pages 36–7). Flatten the paper. The colour should be on the outside.

2 Fold B & C to E.

3 Fold in the corners.

4 (The instructions now refer to B only, but repeat all Steps with C.) Swivel B behind and downwards . . .

 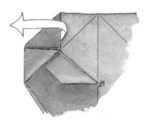  

5 . . . like this . . .

6 . . . and flatten. Unfold.

7 Fold B & C inwards, unfolding the paper to an open square to do this, . . .

8 . . . like this. Re-crease back to Step 6 following Steps 2–6.

9 Note the new shape at B. Fold up triangle B.

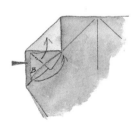

10 Open and squash flat the triangle, forming a square.

11 Swivel the square down and to the right along a hidden crease.

12 Pleat the eye.

13 The Beak complete. Hold as shown and move your hands to and fro to make the mouth open and close!

LIGHTHEARTED

In this design, the final shape is unimpressive, but reveals a translucent heart when held against the light! Use a square of thin paper; thicker papers will not reveal the heart.

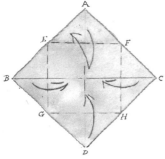

1 Crease and unfold the horizontal diagonal BC. Fold the four corners to the centre.

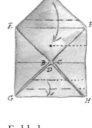

2 Fold down corner A as shown. Pleat triangle DGH as shown.

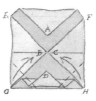

3 Fold in corners G & H. Note the very small intrusion of the crease into the D triangle. This is important, as it affects the proportion of the heart.

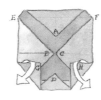

4 Unfold Step 3.

5 Re-crease Step 3, but reverse folding the top part of each crease to push G under B, and H under C.

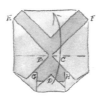

6 Fold in half.

7 Fold in E & F just a little way.

8 Fold over as shown, locking the edges into the pockets made in Step 5.

9 Fold the excess paper into the top pocket.

10 Note that the shape is locked flat.

11 To see the heart, hold the paper up to a window or other diffuse light source (but not the sun).

STAR BOX

It is relatively easy to make a square, straight-sided box, such as the Traditional Box project, but the technical complexities increase as the final shape becomes less plain. This design is pleasingly bold. Use a square of origami paper, with the coloured side outwards.

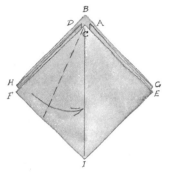

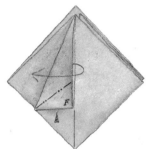

1 Begin with Step 7 of the Star (see pages 34–5), turned upside down. Fold FC to centre.

2 Lift up the single top layer and squash F . . .

3 . . . like this. Fold the outer section of the squash behind.

4 Repeat Steps 2–3 with E.

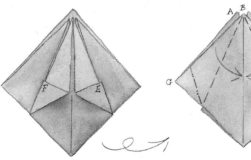

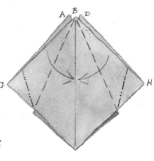

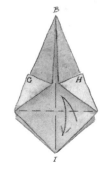

5 Turn over.

6 Repeat Steps 2–4 with G & H.

7 Crease and unfold across the full width of the paper. To help Step 9, the valley can be further creased as a mountain.

8 Fold down B as far as it will go. Repeat with A, C & D.

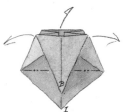

9 Open out the box, flattening the bottom along the Step 7 creases.

10 The Star Box complete.

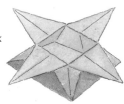

JUMPING FROG

*There are many origami jumping frogs, most – like this one – made by creating
a frog shape, then pleating across the body to create the spring. This version is
a particularly athletic jumper. Use a square of green coloured paper.*

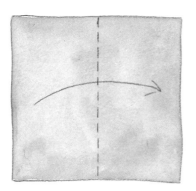

1 Fold a square in half
down the middle.

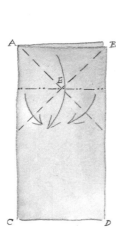

2 The paper is now two
layers thick, but will
be referred to as though it is
a single layer. Collapse AB
to make the shape seen in
Step 6 of the Waterbomb
project (see pages 36–7).

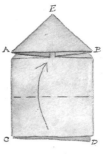

3 Fold up edge CD
to AB.

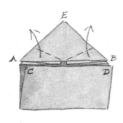 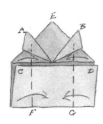 

4 Swing out A & B. Note that they do not touch E, but protrude to the side.

5 Fold in the sides.

6 Fold edge FG to the centre point.

7 Fold down corners F & G . . .

  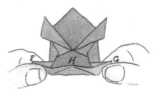 

8 . . . like this.

9 Hold tightly as shown. Slide F & G away from H . . .

10 . . . like this, keeping firm hold of F & G. When F & G have been pulled out as far to the side as they will go, flatten the paper . . .

11 . . . like this. Fold down F & G.

12 Turn over.

13 Make a pleat, with the mountain crease passing through H. The paper is very thick, so apply considerable pressure. But the frog will jump further if the creases are not put in too firmly.

14 The Jumping Frog complete.

15 To make it jump, put your finger on its back. Flatten the pleat and slide your finger off! With practice, it will jump quite a distance.

BIRD

This design is straightforward until Step 9, when the difficult 3D crimp transforms an ordinary flat bird into a 3D bird with a pleasingly rounded shape. Use a square piece of paper, coloured the same on both sides.

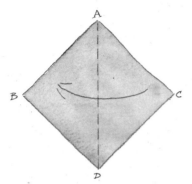

1 Fold C across to B.

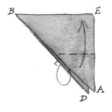

2 Fold A down to D.

3 Fold A up to E. Repeat behind.

4 Fold in the corners.

5 Unfold crease BC,E.

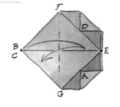

6 Fold BC to E, but creasing halfway from the existing centre crease to corners F & G. Unfold, then re-fold back to step 5.

7 Reverse corners BC & E.

8 Reverse corner C only, creating the open beak.

9 Pull down the triangles front and back as a base for the bird. Crease a mountain fold front and back, so that when folded over the valley made in Step 6, the bird becomes rounded. Unfold the spine a little to assist with this crimp. The bird has to be forced into shape, but will lock strongly when in position. To make the rounded shape push the paper outwards from the inside.

10 The Bird complete.

BUILDING

The design shows how the rectangles and triangles that are created naturally by folding a square along halves and quarters, can be articulated to create a form such as this semi-abstract building, complete with colour-change roofs. Use a square of origami paper, white side up.

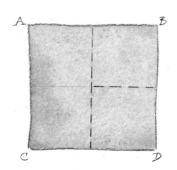

1 Crease as shown. Note the short crease at the right.

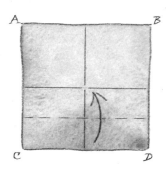

2 Fold edge CD up to the centre crease, then fold in half down the middle.

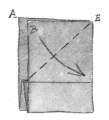

3 Fold down corner B.

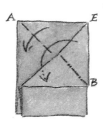

4 Reverse fold corner E behind B.

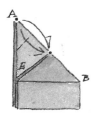

5 Fold corner A as shown, opening the paper to do this.

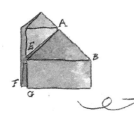

6 Turn over.

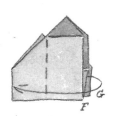

7 Swing F over to
   the left.

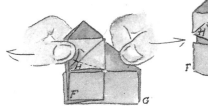

8 Hold as shown and
   move your hands apart.
   Corner H will lift. Crease
   and flatten H as shown . . .

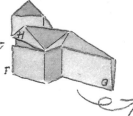

9 . . . like this.
   Turn over.

10 The Building
    complete.

PIG

The Pig, although a fairly complex project, is rewarding to construct, especially when the finished animal emerges as the steps are completed.

1 Crease and unfold the long horizontal centre crease, then crease and unfold the shorter axis.

2 Fold edge AC behind.

3 Fold edge BD behind to the crease made in Step 2.

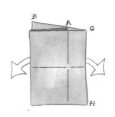

4 Unfold.

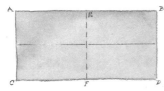

5 Pleat along existing creases EF & GH.

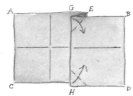

6 Turn in corners G & H.

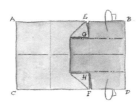

7 Swivel B & D behind, along horizontal mountain creases. Note the shape of Step 8.

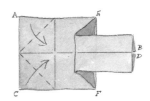

8 Fold in corners A & C.

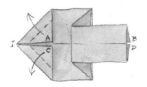

9 Fold A & C back out, the creases tapering towards I.

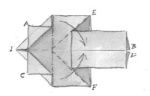

10 Collapse as shown, to make the paper 3D.

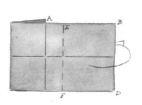

11 Pull out the hidden ledge . . .

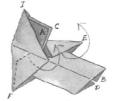

12 . . . and feed it back into the pig between A & C . . .

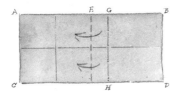

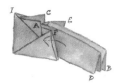

13 . . . like this, bringing F & E back together again.

14 The manoeuvre is complete – its purpose is to stop the pig from splaying its front legs. Turn the paper the right way up.

15 Reverse fold at B & D.

16 Fold B & D towards the neck.

17 Create two reverse folds near the snout, forming a crimp.

18 Fold the snout over and over. Fold the ears forward.

19 Crimp the neck, lowering the head.

20 Pleat the tail.

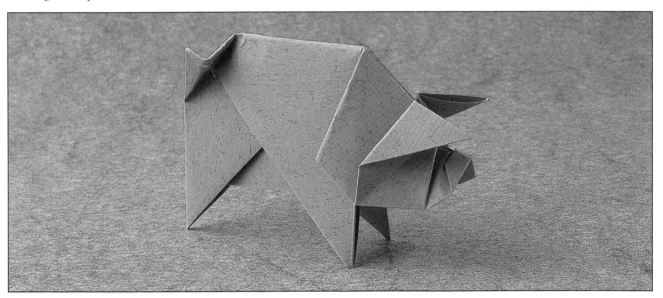

Standing Heart

Hearts are a favourite origami theme. This conventional single heart could make an attractive standing ornament for a mantelpiece or desk top. Use a square of red/white origami paper, red side up.

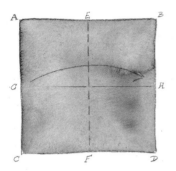
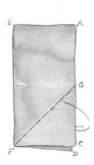

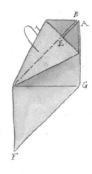

1 Crease and unfold across the middle, then fold AC across to BD.

2 Mountain fold corners C & D inside.

3 Squash fold corner E.

4 Fold the outer section of the squash fold behind.

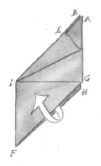
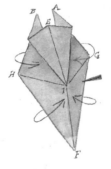
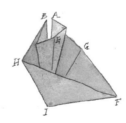

5 Open the paper between G & H. Turn over to see . . .

6 . . . a pyramid. Corner I is the apex (the corner nearest to you). Push on I so that it inverts and the paper pops inside out. Corner I is now the furthest point from you, not the nearest.

7 This is the shape. Note I.

8 Fold down B & A, dot to dot.

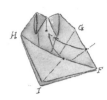
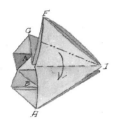
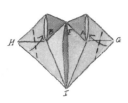

9 Tuck the excess paper into the pockets at B & A.

10 Collapse as shown, folding the two outer dots onto the inner one.

11 Squash F, presently standing upright.

12 Fold in H & G.

13 Fold over G to lock the triangle to the edge behind.

14 Open out the pocket between F & I . . .

15 . . . like this, flattening the paper.

16 Partly close the pocket again. Turn over.

17 The Standing Heart complete.

CHINESE VASE

*This design has a beautifully direct sequence of folds, climaxed by the
extraordinary opening out from 2D to 3D. Use a square of paper,
not too small. If using origami paper, start white side up.*

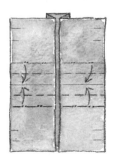

1 Crease a square into eight equal divisions, then
carefully cut off two squares horizontally and
vertically, to create a 6 x 6 grid.

2 Add extra creases
where shown.

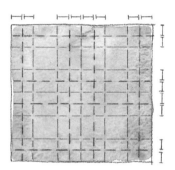

3 Pleat the paper
as shown.

4 Similarly, pleat
horizontally.

5 This is the shape of
the paper. Turn over.

6 This is the shape.

7 Lift and squash the
end of each pleat . . .

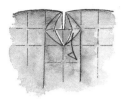

8 . . . like this.

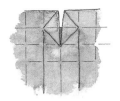

9 Repeat along each edge.

10 Here are the squashed pleats. Turn over.

11 Crease and unfold each loose corner at the pleats. This is to prepare for Step 14.

12 Fold the sides to the middle.

13 Fold the top and bottom edges to the middle, tucking the corners deep into the pockets.

14 Fold the loose corners inside, to create a square opening . . .

15 . . . like this. Turn over.

16 This is the fun part! Carefully tease out the trapped layers inside the pleats to make the vase 3D. Do this by rotating the paper frequently, so that all four sides are developed equally.

17 This is the result. Put a finger into the vase and round out the square, flat corners at the top.

ELECTRA

An appeal of modular folding is that spectacular structures can be made from simple units, so that the whole is very much more than the sum of its parts. Thirty modules are needed for this design. Fold them all carefully, then slot them together, with diligent regard for the "5 and 3" (pentagons and triangles) interlocking pattern. If using origami paper, start with the coloured side up.

1 Crease and unfold both diagonals as valleys. Turn over.

2 Crease and unfold horizontally and vertically. (The diagonals are mountains.)

3 Pinch the quarter points along crease EH.

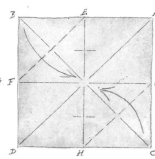

4 Fold corners B & C to the middle.

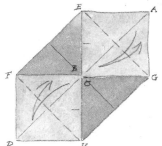

5 Fold and unfold corners A & D.

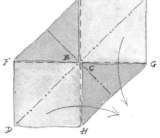

6 Collapse all the creases.

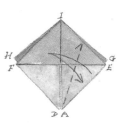

7 Form a crease between A and the pinch made in Step 3, folding E across to the left side. Unfold.

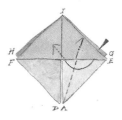

8 Re-form the crease, but reverse fold E inside.

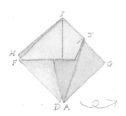

9 This is the result. Turn over.

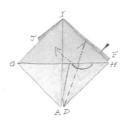

10 Repeat Steps 7–9 with H.

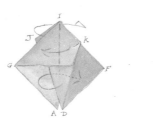

11 Fold K across to the left, allowing the triangle above D to swivel inside and to the right. Repeat behind with J.

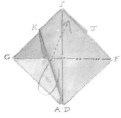

12 Mountain fold D inside, creating a pocket below K. Repeat with A.

13 This is the completed module. Note the closed pockets below J & K and the extended flaps at F & G.

ASSEMBLY

1 Tuck the extended flap on one module (F1), deep inside the pocket of another. To lock them together, fold F or G (depending on which one flap F1 has been tucked into) towards G1.

2 Repeat with the nearside flaps and pockets.

3 Lock 5 modules together, leaving no excess flaps in the centre of the pentagon. A sixth module is shown at the bottom of the drawing connecting two neighbouring pentagon modules, thereby creating a triangle with no loose flaps in its centre. The completed Electra is thus a combination of pentagons and triangles. Interlock the remaining modules following this pattern.

SEAL ON A ROCK

So called "double subjects" or "combination folds" are common in complex
origami, where two subjects or objects are folded from a single sheet.
Use a square of origami paper coloured side up or, for a better effect,
two differently coloured or textured sheets folded back to back.

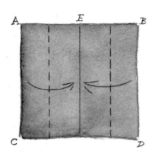   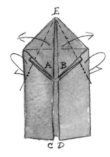

1 Crease and unfold down the centre, then fold the sides to the middle.

2 Reverse fold the top two corners.

3 Collapse, folding A & B downwards and adding the reverse folds.

4 Fold as shown, allowing A & B to swivel outwards.

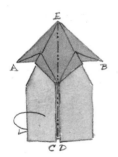 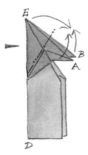  

5 Mountain fold A behind.

6 Reverse fold E, allowing A & B to pivot upwards to touch E.

7 Narrow the paper with two reverse folds.

8 Pleat A & B.

9 Turn E inside out, lowering A & B.

10 Crimp the neck upwards. Release paper for the tail. Repeat behind.

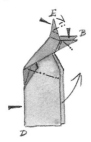

11 Crimp the head. Squash the flippers. Reverse fold the rock.

12 Reverse fold the snout. Round off the flippers. Sink the excess paper inside at the tail.

13 Crimp the rock to make it 3D.

14 The Seal on a Rock complete.

SYMBOLS

No sequence of origami diagrams can be followed without an understanding of the symbols they use. The meaning of most symbols is obvious and it is not necessary to learn them all, but it would be very helpful at least to learn the difference between the mountain and valley fold symbols. The other symbols can be learnt as they appear by referring back to this page.

The same symbols can be found in most origami books, whatever language they are written in, be it English, Spanish or even Japanese.

This standardization means that the language of origami is truly universal, and that enthusiasts can fold from almost any book, East or West.

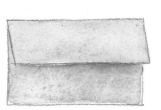 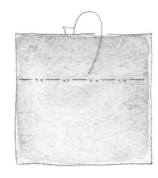 

valley   mountain

turn over   existing creases

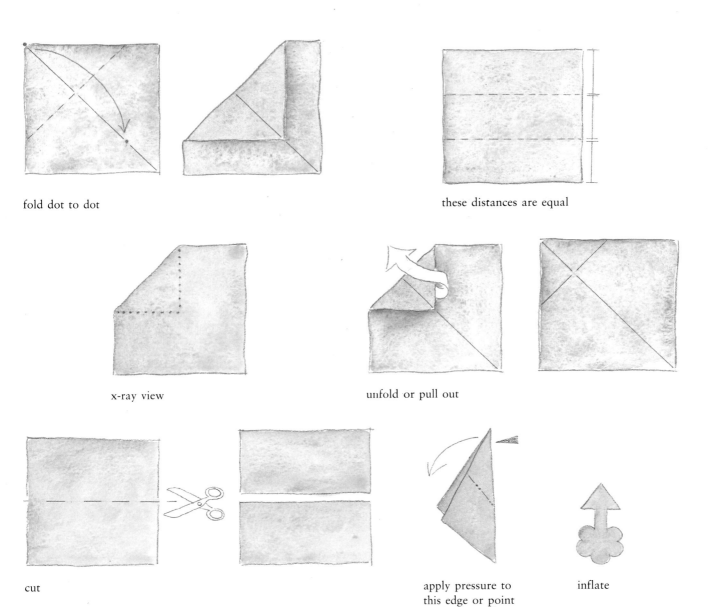

fold dot to dot

these distances are equal

x-ray view

unfold or pull out

cut

apply pressure to
this edge or point

inflate

ADVANCED FOLDING TECHNIQUES

*Apart from the basic mountain and valley creases from which all origami
designs are folded, there are four advanced techniques found in this book. These
techniques are used in combination and are: the squash fold,
the sink fold and the inside and outside reverse folds. However,
not all designs use these advanced techniques.
Squash and sink folds are the least common. To save space, a detailed
explanation of each is given once in the book within a particular design. For an
explanation of the squash fold see the Multiform House, Steps 4–6 (page 30); for an
explanation of the sink fold see the Star, Steps 8–12 (pages 34–5). When you come
across a squash or sink fold in another design, refer to these designs for a
step-by-step guide. Inside and outside reverse folds are not more complex than
squash or sink folds, but are more common and come in a greater variety.
So, to simplify cross-referencing, here are the basic forms of each. Refer to this page
whenever you need to be reminded how to make them.*

INSIDE REVERSE

Pull-through version

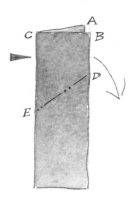

1 This is how the manoeuvre is illustrated in the book.

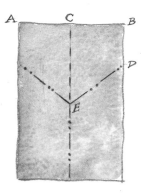

2 This is the crease pattern.

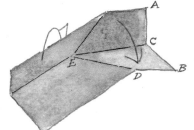

3 Collapse.

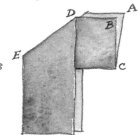

4 Complete.

Push-in version

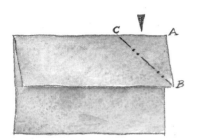

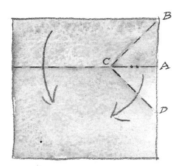

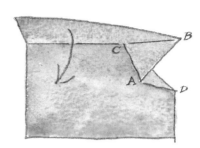

1 This is how the manoeuvre is illustrated in the book.

2 This is the crease pattern.

3 Collapse.

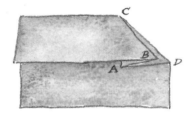

4 Complete.

OUTSIDE REVERSE

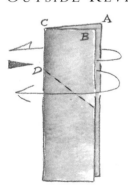

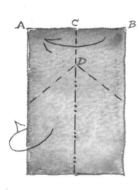

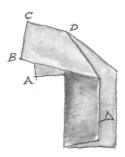

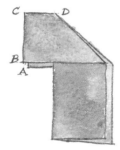

1 This is how the manoeuvre is illustrated in the book.

2 This is the crease pattern.

3 Collapse.

4 Complete.

PAPERCRAFT

We use paper in a variety of ways every day, and some thought and creativity can make many of those uses much more of a pleasure. Next time you want to write a letter, send a card or wrap a gift, think how satisfying it will be, if the paper or card you use is your own unique creation. Hand-made stationery and greetings cards show how much you care, and are bound to be specially appreciated and treasured. There are all kinds of different papers and cards to choose from and it's worth starting a collection of unusual papers to inspire you. You'll find gift ideas in this section ranging from delicate crêpe paper flowers to sturdy papier mâché ornaments. Use these as a starting-point to fire your imagination – you can make almost anything with paper.

CLASSIC LINES

If you want to write a letter in a hurry, but still want it to be stylish,
here are a couple of quick ways to make some beautiful writing paper.
You will need some light-coloured wrapping paper in a classical design.

MATERIALS
....

scissors
pale wrapping paper
tracing paper
glue
sheet of white paper

1 Cut out a rectangle of wrapping paper to the size of the writing paper, and cut a piece of tracing paper the same size. Stick the tracing paper on top of the wrapping paper, smoothing out any bubbles. Use a black felt-tip pen to write your letter so that it shows up clearly.

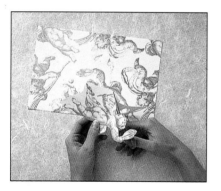

2 If you have a bit more time you could select a motif from the wrapping paper and cut this out.

3 Glue the motif to a sheet of white paper.

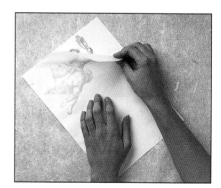

4 As before, glue a sheet of tracing paper on top to give an elegant double layer. You could make a collection of writing paper by cutting out different motifs from one sheet of wrapping paper.

COLLAGE TAGS

When you want to keep things simple and have perhaps used a plain paper
to wrap your present, a collaged gift tag can be the perfect finishing touch.
They can be as easy or as complicated as you want to make them.

1 For the Grecian-style tag cut out a Grecian urn and decorative dots in green paper.

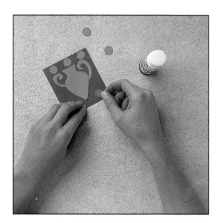

2 Glue them on to a folded piece of orange card.

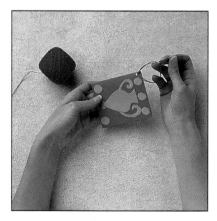

3 Punch a hole and thread through a length of coloured thread or ribbon.

CUT-AND-THREAD PAPER

Make plain writing paper extra special with simple strips of crêpe paper threaded through in unusual patterns. Practise first on spare paper to get the right effect.

sheet of writing paper
pencil
ruler
craft knife
scissors
crêpe paper
envelope

1 Take a sheet of writing paper and mark two sets of two vertical lines at the top, in the centre. The lines should be approximately 2 cm (¾ in) long and 2.5 cm (1 in) apart. Cut through the lines using a craft knife.

2 Cut a piece of crêpe paper in a toning colour to your writing paper. Thread it under the "bridges" taking care not to break them.

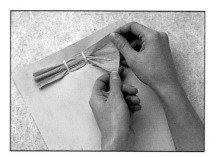

3 Once the crêpe paper is centred, arrange the bow by fanning out the sides.

4 Repeat the bow design on the extended back flap of an envelope to complete the writing set.

5 Another effect can be achieved by marking and cutting out a series of vertical lines across the top of the page. Cut a piece of crêpe paper into a strip the same width as the slots, and a thinner strip in a stronger colour.

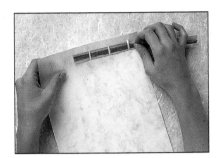

6 Fold the paper in half to thread the strips through easily, and then open up.

7 Instead of using vertical lines, this version uses two staggered lines of horizontal slits. Once again, thread the strip of crêpe paper through and see the diagonal pattern it makes.

21ST BIRTHDAY POP-UP

This unusual card is perfect for celebrating a special birthday. Once you have mastered the simple pop-up technique you could use different numbers for a variety of important birthdays.

MATERIALS

pencil
plain paper
stiff white paper
craft knife
poster paints and paintbrush
glue
stiff coloured paper

1 Scale up the "21" shape to the size required and transfer to a piece of stiff white paper. Cut it out using a craft knife and paint the numbers. When the paint is dry, fold the "21" shape in half and glue the underside of each tab.

2 Next, fold a piece of stiff coloured paper in two to form a card shape. Glue one tab to one half of the backing card, so that the bottom of the crease down the middle of the "21" exactly touches the crease on the card.

3 To finish off, apply glue to the second tab and fold the empty half of the backing card over the top of the second tab. When unfolded, the card will stick to this second tab, pulling up the "21". Decorate the base card.

WRAPPING A SPHERE

*A sphere-shaped present is always a difficult shape to wrap up and it can
be approached in two ways. The gift can either be placed in the centre of
a piece of paper which can then be gathered up into a bunch above the
present and tied with ribbon, or the paper can be pleated, as here.*

MATERIALS
....

*sphere-shaped present
wrapping paper
scissors
sticky tape
double-sided tape*

1 Place the present in the centre
of a square piece of wrapping
paper. Make the square into a circle
by rounding off the corners.

2 Start by bringing one section of
the paper up to the top. Now
work around the circle by pleating
the paper so that it hugs the shape of
the sphere. Use sticky tape to secure
the pleats as you go round.

3 Continue to pleat neatly until
you have gone all the way
around. To finish, make a pleated
fan. Fold a strip of paper in half
with the right side outside. Pleat the
paper along its length.

4 Then, pinch the pleats together
at the bottom and fan out the
sides. Attach it to the present by
fixing with double-sided tape.

TAG TIME

Make your own gift tags for a personal touch as well as to save money. Used greetings cards can often be cut down and made into brand-new gift tags. Another idea is to take a motif from the wrapping paper used to cover your present.

MATERIALS

scissors
wrapping paper or greetings cards
glue
thin card
ribbon

1 When you have wrapped the present, cut out a suitable motif from the spare paper. Glue the motif on to some thin card in a co-ordinating colour.

2 Following the shape of the motif, cut around the design so that the card forms a border.

3 Now punch a hole in the card with a scissor blade and thread a ribbon through the hole. Write a message on the tag and attach it to the present.

STAND-UP PLACE NAMES

Make your place cards really stand out with these novelty motifs that project above the cards.

MATERIALS

green, orange, red and white card
scissors
glue
gold metallic pen
craft knife

1 Fold a square of green card in half. Cut out an octopus from the orange card and position it so the top half is above the fold line. Cut out the facial features from the green card and glue in place.

2 For a festive place name, cut out two holly leaves in green. Stick them on to the top of a red place card so that the holly is sticking upwards. Cut out and glue on red dots for the berries.

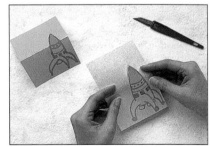

3 To make the rocket, mark the fold line on the card and lay it flat. Draw the rocket with gold pen so that the top extends over the fold line. With a craft knife, cut around the top part only. Then fold the card and the rocket will stand up.

SECRET MESSAGES

Give a sense of mystery to your gifts by adding a tag tied with a ribbon bow to
conceal your message. A perfect idea for sending notes to loved ones.

MATERIALS

coloured card
craft knife
ruler
contrasting coloured paper
gold metallic pen
glue
gold ribbon

1 Take a rectangle of card and fold in half. Open out the card and make a small narrow slit for the ribbon on the centre of both leading edges, back and front.

2 On a separate piece of contrasting paper draw a design with a gold pen and stick this on to the card.

3 Write your message inside and then thread a length of gold ribbon through the slits and tie a bow to keep the wording a secret.

CANDY CONES

*Pretty and simple ideas for arranging candies at a wedding or party. For an
alternative, wrap a red ribbon upwards around a cone made from elegant
wrapping paper and use matching red tissue paper inside.*

MATERIALS

*20 cm (8 in) square of wrapping paper
glue
rosette
tissue paper
sugared almonds or candies*

1 Roll the square of wrapping
paper into a cone, starting
with a corner and shaping it into a
rounded form.

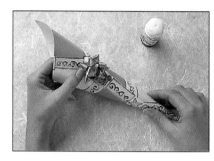

2 Glue the cone together along the
edge and stick a rosette on the
overlapping point. Flatten the cone at
the closed end.

3 Scrunch up some matching tissue
paper and push this into the
open end. Fill with sugared almonds
or candies.

You can vary the design of the cones, depending on the occasion, using different paper and ribbons.

MATERIALS

scissors
black and gold paper
pencil
glue
ribbon or bow
tissue paper
chocolate coins

1 For a variation, cut one square in black paper and another in gold paper. Zigzag the edges along two adjacent sides of the black square, first drawing a line about 1.5 cm (¾ in) from the edge as a guideline.

2 Then glue the black paper on to the gold paper and roll up into a cone form, gluing along the edges where they overlap.

3 Slightly flatten the end of the cone and stick on a bow or pieces of ribbon.

4 Take some contrasting tissue paper and scrunch it up and insert it into the cone. Fill with chocolate coins.

GIFT BAG

This gift bag is simple to make and adds a touch of elegance to any present. It can be used instead of separate wrapping paper and is sturdy enough to hold a variety of gifts.

MATERIALS
....

pencil
paper
ruler
decorated paper
craft knife
glue
hole punch
scissors
ribbon

1 Scale up the template using pencil, paper and a ruler to the size required and transfer the pattern on to the decorated paper. Cut out carefully using a craft knife. Score lightly along the back of the creases so that they will fold more easily. Fold down and glue the flaps along the top edge of the bag.

2 Next, glue the long side tab to form the bag shape.

3 Then glue the base of the bag in position, folding in the short end tabs first.

4 Form the pleats down the sides of the bag by pressing the long edges together gently so that the paper is pushed inwards.

5 Using the hole punch, make two holes on each of the top sides near the upper edge. Cut two short lengths of ribbon and thread each end through the holes to make two looped handles. Knot the ends at the back of the holes to secure.

STENCIL STYLE

Use ready-made stencils or cut your own to make this stylish writing paper.
Dab on stencil paints or colour with soft crayons for speedy results.

MATERIALS
....

pencil
stencilling card
craft knife
paint
saucer
stencil brush
writing paper
crayon

1 Using the template and a pencil, transfer the motif on to stencilling card in the size you need and cut out using a craft knife.

2 Prepare the paint on a saucer and collect the colour on to a stencil brush. Then, holding the stencilling card firmly, dab the brush on to the writing paper using a circular movement.

3 Instead of using paint, a coloured crayon could be used. Once again, hold the stencilling card firmly and lightly fill in the pattern, remembering to work all the crayon strokes in the same direction for a neat finish.

PAPER QUILLS

The old-fashioned papercraft known as quilling is used to make this distinctive
card. You can design a picture in the same way, and hang it on the wall.

MATERIALS

scissors
assorted coloured papers
strong clear glue
contrasting coloured card

1 Cut long narrow strips of
various shades of coloured paper.
First curl one end of each strip with
the blunt edge of a pair of scissors,
then, starting at this end, roll the
strip into a tight coil.

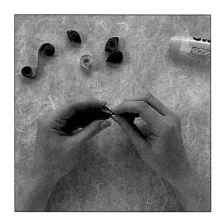

2 Release the coil slightly and
glue the end. Hold this in
position until the glue is dry. Pinch
the outside of the coils between your
fingers to form different shapes such
as a pear, scroll or eye.

3 Fold a rectangular piece of card
in a contrasting colour in half.
Arrange the shaped quills on the card
and stick down, spreading the glue
on the bottom edge of each quill.

BEAUTIFUL BINDING

*If you have an old book or album which you want to brighten up, you can learn
how to cover your own pages. For this project you will need to determine
the size of your book.*

*ruler
craft knife
book or photograph album
thick card
adhesive cloth tape
glue
patterned and plain wrapping paper
pencil
hole punch
cord*

1 First cut two pieces of thick card
that are about 1 cm (½ in) wider
and longer than the pages to be
covered. If you are covering a loose-
leaf album, measure the side strip of
the album sheet which has the holes
punched in it, and mark the same
amount on to the top of one of the
cards, which will eventually be the
top cover. Cut a small strip off one
side of this.

2 Using the other back card as a
measure, place the trimmed top
card on it and put the narrow strip
above so that there is a gap between
them where the strip has been
removed. Tape the pieces together
using adhesive cloth tape. Turn the
block over and put another piece of
the cloth tape on the other side, thus
making the hinge for the top cover.

3 Now glue on a sheet of
decorative paper to cover the
outsides. Glue a toning or contrasting
plain colour to cover the inside.

4 Next lay an album or page sheet on to the bottom cover and draw where the holes are on it. Punch them through using a hole punch. Repeat the process with the front cover.

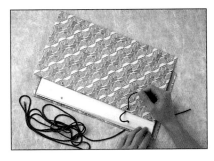

5 Now place the pages on to the back cover so that the holes are aligned and put the front cover on top. To finish off, thread a good quality cord through the holes.

ANTIQUE MARBLING

*There are several methods of marbling paper to achieve the beautiful effects
seen on old bookbinding and traditional Italian stationery. The process
involves suspending pigment on the surface of water, arranging the colour into
patterns, and transferring these to paper.*

MATERIALS

*metal roasting pan or deep tray
cold water
scissors
paper
oil paints in various colours
white spirit
paintbrush or metal skewer*

1 Half fill a clean metal roasting
pan or a deep tray with cold
water. Cut a piece of paper to fit the
size of the container. Thin a little oil
paint with white spirit, and dot the
diluted paint on to the surface of the
water with a brush or skewer.

2 The paint will disperse, creating
patterns on the surface of the
water. Hold the paper by the top
right- and bottom left-hand corners
and lower it across the surface of the
water in a rolling movement.

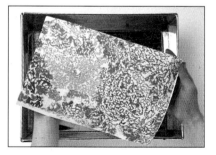

TIP
Before marbling subsequent pieces of
paper, skim the surface of the water
with scrap paper to pick up excess
paint and keep the water clean.

3 Carefully lift the paper from the
container. The paint will adhere
to the paper, giving a marbled effect.
Lay the sheets out to dry at room
temperature.

4 To create multi-coloured patterns
add more colours to the water.
Use a paintbrush or metal skewer
to move the colours around before
laying down the paper.

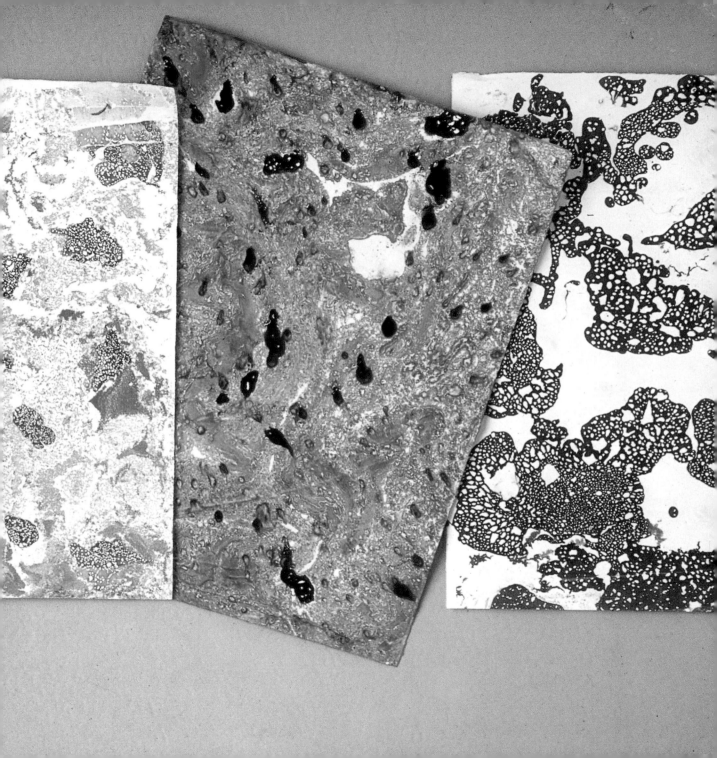

ONE-PIECE GIFT BOXES

This box is constructed from a single piece of card and can be closed tightly, making it an ideal container, either vertical or horizontal, for candies or small biscuits.

MATERIALS

pencil
thin card
craft knife
glue

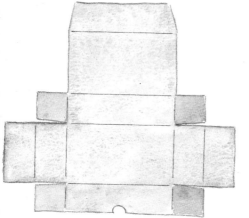

1 Scale up the template to the size required, and transfer it to the card. Cut it out using a craft knife. Score along the back folds of the tabs. Fold up the sides of the box and glue the end tab to make a tube shape.

2 Interlock the tabs at the base of the box; it should lock securely without the use of glue.

VALENTINE'S HEART

This pop-up surprise will add a touch of fun to Valentine's Day. The same technique can be used to make cards for other occasions, such as a tree for Christmas time, or a house for a friend's moving day.

MATERIALS

pencil
scissors
stiff paper in red and cream
glue
red felt-tip pen

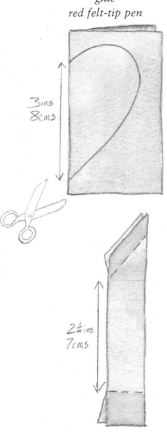

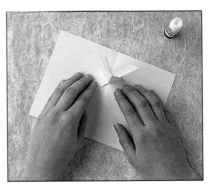

1 Scale up the support from the template to the required size and cut out of a piece of stiff paper. Then fold a matching piece of paper into two halves to form a card. Fold the support to the correct shape, creasing the tabs upwards.

2 Next, glue the support to the backing card near the top, ensuring that the crease on the support exactly touches the crease on the card. Note that the support is symmetrically placed over the crease.

3 Cut out a heart shape in red paper and glue it to the tabs at the top of the support. Decorate the inside border of the card to match with the felt-tip pen. When the card is opened the heart will spring out, giving the recipient a lovely surprise!

NOTELET HOLDER

*Take an ordinary writing pad and envelopes and dress them up
in a special notelet holder. All kinds of versions are possible,
made from decorative papers and cards.*

*writing paper and envelopes
pencil
scissors
card
ruler
glue
brown paper or wrapping paper
gold metallic pen
craft knife
2 paper fasteners
string*

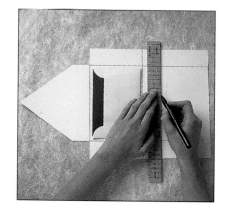

1 To make the notelet holder use one of the envelopes to determine the size, and cut a piece of card, measuring the length of the envelope and adding 8 cm (3 in), by three times the height of the envelope plus 8 cm (3 in).

2 Cut out the card with or without the pointed flap according to the finished style that you require.

3 Apply glue to the unmarked side of the cut-out card, and then cover in brown paper, trimming the edges where necessary. Taking a gold pen, draw a design on to the brown paper.

4 On the inside, score along the marked lines with a craft knife and cut the tab lines.

5 To make the notelets, take six sheets of paper from the writing pad and glue a piece of brown paper or wrapping paper on to each sheet. Trim to size.

6 Decorate the brown paper with the gold pen as before. Fold the paper in half and pop the six notelets and envelopes into the notelet holder.

7 Fold and glue the holder. Push the fasteners through the flap in the front of the box. Secure the case with a loop of string round each of the fasteners.

CONCENTRIC TWIST

Hang this impressive paper sculpture in a window; if it is made from metallic-coated card it will catch the light as it moves gently in the air currents.

pencil
thin coloured card
craft knife

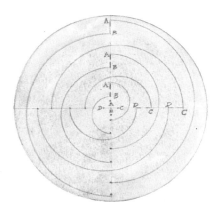

1 Scale up the template to the required size and transfer to coloured card. Cut the slits using a craft knife. Gently twist the outer circle away from its frame.

2 Starting at the rim, form the first twist by gently turning the central section at an angle of 90 degrees to the outer ring.

3 Continue to form the twists by turning each ring at the same angle, moving progressively towards the centre, until the twist-out is finally complete.

PERFORMING PIERROT

Children will love to watch the clever movements of this traditional Pierrot puffet. Why not make a couple and put on a show?

MATERIALS

pencil
blue, white and red paper
scissors
black felt-tip pen
glue
4 paper fasteners
metal skewer or scissor blade
thin string
curtain ring

1 Scale up the pieces from the template to the size required and transfer to the coloured paper. Cut out the shapes for the clown: one body, two legs, two arms and a hat in blue; collar, cuffs and pom-poms in white. Mark on reference dots with a black pen. First make up the face by gluing on his hat and rosy cheeks. Draw the face details in with the black felt-tip pen.

2 Glue the pom-poms on to the hat, front and Pierrot's boots, and stick on the collar and cuffs.

3 Match up the dots on the body and the limbs and join them all together by gently pushing the paper fasteners through both layers. Open out the fasteners on the back.

4 On the reverse side, pull the limbs downwards and pierce a hole at the top of each arm using a skewer or scissor blade. Thread a length of thin string through each hole and knot at both ends on the reverse side. Repeat this with the legs to form two "cross bars".

5 Thread a long piece of string through a curtain ring. Attach one end to the centre of the arm string and the other end to the centre of the leg string. Trim if necessary. The strings should not be slack when the limbs are "at rest". When the strings are firmly fixed, pull the ring and watch Pierrot perform.

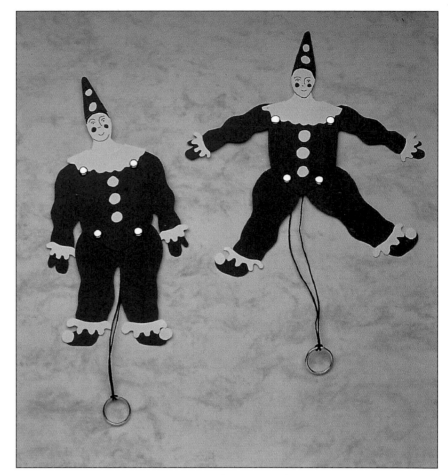

A GREAT CATCH

This handsome fish is displayed proudly on a papier mâché stand, rather like a trophy. It would be fun to make a papier mâché case displaying a similar "catch" to hang on the wall!

MATERIALS

pencil
heavy corrugated card
scissors or craft knife
strong clear glue
masking tape
newspaper
diluted PVA (white) glue
fine sandpaper
paintbrush
white paint
poster paints
black ink (optional)
non-toxic clear gloss varnish

1 Scale up the fish shape and stand from the template to the required size, and transfer on to the corrugated card. Cut out two pieces for the stand. Stick the two halves of the stand together with strong clear glue, hold the joins with masking tape and leave to dry.

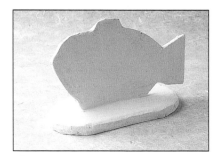

3 Lightly sand down the fish and stand. Prime with white paint.

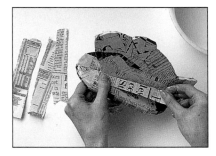

2 Soak newspaper strips in diluted PVA (white) glue and apply three layers of papier mâché to the fish and stand. Leave them to dry overnight in a warm place.

4 Draw in the fish's face, fins and other features, and then decorate it with poster paints. Use black ink to draw in the detail, if required. Let the fish dry overnight and then seal it with two coats of clear gloss varnish.

POPULAR POPPIES

*The stark simplicity of bright red poppies with their black centres
makes them an ideal flower to craft in paper.*

MATERIALS

*scissors
garden wire
cotton wool (surgical cotton)
green, black and red crêpe paper
sticky tape
glue*

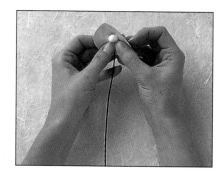

1 To make the stem, cut a length of garden wire. Bend the top to make a loop and trap a small amount of cotton wool (surgical cotton) in the loop. Cover this in a cut-out circle of green crêpe paper. Secure by wrapping tape around it.

2 Next cut three small circles of black crêpe paper. Fringe the outer edges and then poke the other end of the wire through the centre and slide up to the green bud.

3 Cut out five petal shapes in red crêpe paper and stretch the outer edges with your fingertips so that they frill.

4 Glue the petals one by one around the base of the centre.

5 Finally, cover the stem in green crêpe paper by winding a long strip around diagonally and securing it at the base with sticky tape.

ELEGANT LAMPSHADE

*Add a designed look to your room by using a leftover piece of wallpaper,
or a paper of a complementary colour, to make this lampshade.*

MATERIALS

*lampshade frame
coloured paper or wallpaper
pen
scissors or craft knife
coin
glue*

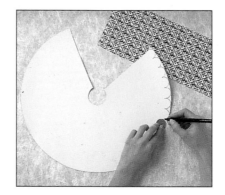

1 Take a lampshade frame and place it on to your chosen paper. Draw around the shape while slowly moving the frame round to obtain the correct measurement. Now cut out the shape slightly outside the drawn line using scissors or a craft knife to give a piece of paper larger than the frame. Using a coin, draw a scalloped edge along the bottom of the paper.

2 Then cut along it until the edging is complete.

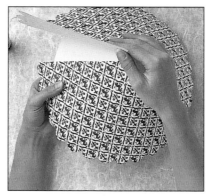

3 Now apply a layer of glue to the frame and carefully attach the paper to it, smoothing it out to avoid bumps or creases.

4 Finally, cut small darts around the top and glue them down, working around until the frame is completely covered and the shade ready to be fitted to a lamp.

WASTE PAPER BASKET

*Découpage decoration quickly covers surfaces in beautiful and unusual designs.
It is particularly effective on shiny materials, such as this metal waste paper basket.*

MATERIALS

*flat brush
diluted PVA (white) glue
metal waste paper basket
pale blue and yellow tissue paper
scissors
flowery wrapping paper
clear polyurethane varnish*

1 Brush dilute PVA (white) glue liberally all over the basket.

2 Tear long strips of tissue paper and paste them round the middle area of the basket.

3 Cut out an assortment of strips and motifs from wrapping paper. Decide on the design of the basket and dip the pieces of wrapping paper in PVA (white) glue. Stick them on to the basket according to your design and brush them flat. Add more strips of the tissue paper until the design is complete. Leave to dry. Finish with a final coat of glue and leave to dry. Finally, cover with a coat of clear polyurethane varnish and leave to dry.

DESIGNER PENCIL POT

This pencil pot is a lovely idea to cheer up your own desk, or it can make a beautiful personalized gift for a friend. The matching pencils add an artistic touch.

MATERIALS

empty cardboard tube or
salt container
tape measure
pencil
scissors
patterned paper
glue

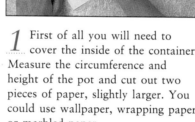

1 First of all you will need to cover the inside of the container. Measure the circumference and height of the pot and cut out two pieces of paper, slightly larger. You could use wallpaper, wrapping paper or marbled paper.

2 Take one of the pieces, glue it and carefully slot it into the inside of the pot, pressing it around the inside walls.

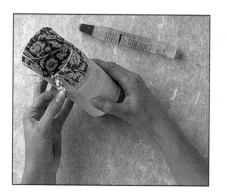

3 Cut darts on the excess paper at the top and glue them down to the outside one by one.

4 Take the other piece of paper and stick it to the outside so that the edge is flush with the top of the pot.

5 Once again cut darts into the excess length at the bottom and glue them on to the base.

6 Now draw around the base of the pot on to the patterned paper and cut out a circle slightly smaller. Glue this and drop it inside the pot and fix to the base.

7 Cut out another circle and glue it to the outside base. To make the matching pencils, cut out a strip of the patterned paper the length of the pencils and approximately three times the width. Glue it and place the pencil at one edge and roll it up. Trim the paper where necessary.

DESK BLOTTER

To make the blotter special it is a good idea to select a wrapping paper to suit the type of desk area. You could choose a hand-made marbled paper for a very traditional look, or an abstract paper or two co-ordinating plain papers for a more modern effect.

MATERIALS

scissors
thick card
patterned paper
glue
thin card
coloured paper
blotting paper

1 Cut a piece of thick card 45 x 30 cm (18 x 12 in). This will be the size of the blotter. Cut your chosen paper 2.5 cm (1 in) larger all round than the card.

2 Next fold and glue the edges of the paper on to the back of the card, mitring the corners by trimming them diagonally.

3 For the corner pieces cut four triangles in thin card measuring 10 x 10 x 14 cm (4 x 4 x 5½ in) and cover them in coloured paper 2.5 cm (1 in) bigger all round. Glue and turn down the bottom edge and the top point. Repeat for all corner pieces.

4 Position the corner pieces on to the corners of the blotter. Turn the board over and fold the edges around, gluing them securely.

5 Cut another piece of coloured paper the same size as the blotter and glue it on to the back. Trim where necessary.

6 Insert a piece of blotting paper under the corners.

TIP
For a co-ordinated desk, why not make the designer pencil pot on pages 114–15 to match the blotter.

SPARKLING FRAME

This frame is decorated with two different coloured foils, and will take standard-sized photographs. It opens at the side and could easily be made larger to accommodate bigger pictures.

MATERIALS

pencil
heavy corrugated cardboard
thin corrugated cardboard
scissors
strong clear glue
masking tape
diluted PVA (white) glue
2 picture hangers
newspaper
fine sandpaper
paintbrush
white paint
silver foil
gold foil
cord for hanging

1 Scale up the frame pieces from the template to the size you require. Transfer the front to heavy cardboard and the spacer to thin cardboard. Cut a rectangle in heavy cardboard to form the back of the frame. Stick the spacer to three sides of the reverse of this rectangle with strong clear glue and then secure with tape. One side is left open for inserting the picture. When dry, prime the pieces with diluted PVA (white) glue to help prevent warping. Allow to dry for four hours. Glue and tape the hangers to the back.

2 Soak newspaper strips about 2.5 cm (1 in) wide in diluted PVA (white) glue. Cover both pieces of frame with three layers of papier mâché. Let it dry overnight, and then sand the layers lightly with fine sandpaper.

3 Prime the frame pieces with two coats of white paint before they are joined. Although the paint will eventually be covered, you will be able to see much more easily where to stick the foil if the surface of the frame is white. Stick the back to the front of the frame with strong clear glue, and hold the joins together with tape. Cover the joins with two layers of papier mâché strips, and when dry, apply another coat of white paint.

4 To decorate the frame, cut strips of silver foil to fit on the frame and glue them in place. Make sure that you cover the inside edges of the frame. Next, cut shapes from gold foil and stick them around the frame. Finally, attach some cord to the back of the frame, around the hangers.

MONOCHROME DÉCOUPAGE

Découpage is the traditional art of decorating surfaces with paper cut-outs of
Victorian-style images. This project has a contemporary feel, however, by using
monochrome cut-outs and a modern box covered in brown paper.

MATERIALS

black-and-white pictures
scissors
card or wooden box
glue
varnish (if needed)

1 Start by choosing your images.
The ones used here are from
wrapping paper. Cut them out
carefully following their outlines.

2 Arrange the images on a box
and then glue them into position.
A card gift box is used here but you
could apply the paper cut-outs to a
wooden box such as an old cigar box.
If you choose a wooden box, you
would need to coat the decorated box
with a layer of varnish.

TWIRLING PARROTS MOBILE

The movement of these colourful twirling parrots will fascinate young children.

pencil
tracing paper
thick card
scissors
poster paints
paintbrush
coloured ribbon in 3 colours
dowelling

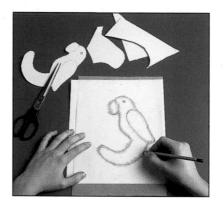

1 Scale up the parrot template to the size required and trace on to thick card. Cut out carefully using scissors. Trace and cut out three parrot shapes.

2 Paint the parrots in a variety of bright colours and leave to dry completely.

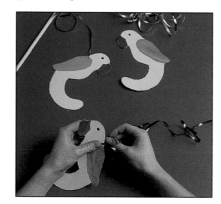

3 Pierce a small hole in the back of each parrot's neck and thread through a piece of coloured ribbon. Knot the end to secure and tie the other end to the dowelling. Space the parrots evenly along the dowelling, varying the lengths of ribbon to create a balanced effect. Suspend the mobile by tying a length of ribbon around the centre of the dowelling.

"Baroque" Christmas Wreath

The base for this beautiful wreath is an embroidery hoop. An oval one is used here but a round one would work just as well.

Materials

scissors
gold crêpe paper
glue
oval embroidery hoop
gold card
paintbrush or pencil
black felt-tip pen

1 Cut a long strip of gold crêpe paper and glue one end to the hoop. Wind the paper around the hoop to cover it completely.

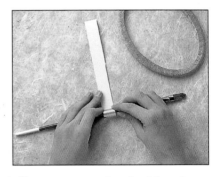

2 Now cut a strip of gold card approximately 1 x 30 cm (½ x 12 in) and wrap it tightly around a paintbrush or pencil.

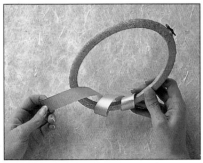

3 Attach one end of the curled gold strip halfway up the right-hand side of the hoop, wind around the hoop and fix the other end just beyond the bottom point.

4 Using the template, scaled to the size required, draw the angel playing the trumpet on to the back of some gold card and cut out. Draw on the features with a black felt-tip pen. Make a bow out of gold crêpe paper and stick it on to the top of the wreath.

5 Now fix the angel to the left-hand side of the wreath.

TREE DECORATIONS

Good, unusual Christmas decorations are often hard to find. If you want an alternative to glittery baubles then you may like to make these decorations from papier mâché, or you could design your own.

pencil
tracing paper
thin card
craft knife
small metal jewellery hangers,
one for each decoration
strong clear glue
masking tape
newspaper
diluted PVA (white) glue
fine sandpaper
paintbrush
white paint
pencil
assortment of poster paints
black ink (optional)
non-toxic clear gloss varnish
cord to hang decorations

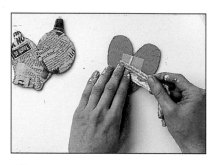

1 Trace the decoration shapes from the template, scaling up to the size required, and transfer them to the thin card. Cut out each shape. Stick a hanger on to the back of each decoration with strong clear glue, and hold it in place with masking tape.

2 Allow the glue to dry for an hour, and then cover each decoration with three layers of small, thin newspaper strips soaked in diluted PVA (white) glue. Leave to dry in a warm place overnight.

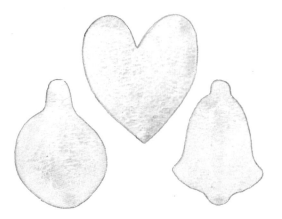

3 Then sand the dry decorations lightly with fine sandpaper, and prime each one with two coats of white paint.

4 Draw in your design with pencil, and then colour your decorations with poster paints. Define details with black ink, if required. Allow the decorations to dry, and then seal them with two coats of clear gloss varnish. When they are dry, tie a loop of cord to the top of each decoration.

INDEX